Mama's Slippers

A Play In Two Acts

by
Jim Melanson

MAMA'S SLIPPERS
A Play in Two Acts

Melanson Publishing,
Newcastle, Ontario
www.melansonpublishing.ca

First Published 2014
ISBN: 978-0-9937565-2-8

Printed by CreateSpace, an Amazon.com Company
Available from Amazon.com and other online stores.

For more information and other titles visit
www.melansonpublishing.ca

Music Acknowledgement

"*Mother Machree*" performed by John McDermott. Music by Ernest R. Ball, Chauncey Olcott. Lyrics by Rida Jonson-Young. Dedicated to Jean V. Critchlow. ©Dalriada Publishing Ltd. All Rights Reserved.

"*Living Years*" © Virgin Records. Performed by Mike And The Mechanics. All Rights Reserved.

"*Bridge Over Troubled Waters*" ©1969 Paul Simon. Performed by Paul Simon. All Rights Reserved.

"*You're Sixteen*" ©Mijac Music, Warner-Tamerlane Publishing Corp., Written by Richard M. Sherman & Robert B. Sherman. All Rights Reserved.

"*Frère Jacques*". Unknown origin, is in the public domain.

*It is up to each individual production to secure the performance rights for the lyrics/music to he above songs.

Cast of Characters

MIKE LANE
Man in his late 40's. Always has a pair of women's
slippers in his jacket pocket.

MOM IN HER 20'S
Jet black long hair, pretty in a plain Jane sort of way. She wears a pair
of slippers identical to the ones in Mikes pocket.

MOM IN HER 30'S
Similar looking woman if possible. Shorter hair, has put on weight.
Wears a pair of women's slippers identical to the ones Mom In Her
20's is wearing.

MOM IN HER 40'S
Similar looking woman if possible. Short hair still, put on a bit more
weight. Wears a pair of women's slippers identical to the ones Mom In
Her 20's is wearing.

VERY YOUNG MIKE
In reality, about three years old. Can be played by an older child so
long as Seven Year Old Mike looks older than this child.

SEVEN YEAR OLD MIKE

In reality, seven or eight years old. Can be played by a child up to about ten years old, so long as he isn't too tall. Wears typical kids clothes.

TEENAGE MIKE

Fifteen years old. Has short hair, very clean cut looking.

NANNY REID

Woman in her late 50's or early 60's. Is in a wheelchair. Has poor eye-sight.

MIKES FATHER

Male in his early 30's. Clean cut looking. Hair is always well groomed and parted on the side. Typical 60's look.

UNCLE #1

Male in his late 20's. Doubles as one of the orderlies in the opening sequence.

UNCLE #2

Male in his mid 30's. Doubles as one of the orderlies in the opening sequence.

ACT 1

(House lights go down, stage is in darkness. From back stage we can hear a young childs voice singing A Capella)

Frère Jacques,
Frère Jacques,
Dormer-vous?
Dormer-vous?
Sonner le matin,
Sonner le matin,
Ding-ding-dong,
(this last line said slower)
Ding-ding-dong

(During the song, spotlight is slowly coming up on lower centre stage. Light is fully up as child finishes singing, very brief pause, sound of a door opening and closing. Mike Lane slowly walks out on stage with his hands in his pockets, staring at the floor, lost in thought and stops in the spotlight. Stands there for a moment with his hands in his pockets, looks up suddenly realizing he might not be alone. Puts his hand up to his forehead to shade his eyes and peers into the darkness)

MIKE LANE:

Hello? Is anyone there? Hello? Well, I suppose you're there. I mean, the stage manager told me it was time to go on and she wouldn't have done that if there was no one here.

(Sigh and pause)

I want to thank you all for being here with me. It's not easy when you mother passes away. I appreciate you being here. I do. Really. I mean, I probably don't know any of you. I might though. Jim? Are you there? Cheryl? Judy?

(Pause, appears to be fighting back tears)

I'm sorry, just a moment please.

(Takes a moment to compose himself)

Okay. My mother died tonight. Just a few minutes ago actually.

("Mother Machree" by John McDermott starts playing softly in the background. Weak spotlight comes up on back of stage and we see two orderlies pushing a gurney through the light with a covered body on it, light fades as they pass out of it, Mike Lane continues, music still low volume and the song plays to it's conclusion faintly in the background as Mike Lane speaks)

Yep. I was holding her hand when it happened. When she passed I mean. I felt a little, a little tremble in her fingers. I stood up out of my chair and leaned over her. She had a little smile on her face while I stood looking at her. I reached over and smoothed her hair. She whispered something so I leaned in close and she said it again. "Eddie's here".

(Starts to cry, dabs his eyes with a hankie)

Eddie was my father. He died over thirty years ago. Then she just looked at me and *(pause)* the light went out of her eyes.

(Composes himself again, reaches in his jacket pocket and takes a pair of women's slippers out of them).

These were her slippers. After she passed, I saw them on the floor by her bed. I knew she'd be upset if she lost them.

(Sort of playing with slippers and looking into the audience, trying to make it seem like no big deal but it's a very big deal)

Mom always needed to know where her slippers were. They always had to be lined up by her bed at night. When she went out of the house, they were always lined up by the door. When she packed to go anywhere, the last thing into the suitcase and the first thing out of it was her slippers. I think I only saw her once without her slippers on in the house and that was because she was in bed, took short and had to run to the bathroom. *(laughs quietly)* I think that mom always believed that no matter what happened, so long as you had your slippers, *(pause)* you had your shit together.

(Looks frustrated and a bit angry, shoves the slippers back into his jacket pocket, pauses a moment, breaks down in tears and takes a couple seconds to cry and then compose himself again).

I'm sorry folks. I guess some of you know what this is like, losing your mom. My wife told me that this way was better. She said that her lingering death made it easier for me to deal with it and say my good byes. I told her she was full of shit and didn't know what she was talking about. Her mothers still alive, God bless her. I knew there was no way in hell she could understand what it's like to lose your mother. To sit there and watch her slowly wasting away, knowing the end was coming but not knowing when it was going to arrive. I didn't think she knew anything. Guess she did though. Guess she really did know better than me. You may wonder why she's not here with me tonight. My wife I mean, not my mother. She's working. I really thought mom had a few weeks left. I guess that really, I just wanted her to have a few weeks more. Carol wanted to come with me tonight, she was going to take the night off work and come with me but I told her, I told her not to. I said tonight's not the night. It really wasn't the night either *(pause)* but it was. Nurse Hollinger has been a sweetheart, an angel. She knew. She knew it was the night. She ordered up a couple sandwiches and some coffee for me so I wouldn't have to go to the cafeteria. I didn't realize till just a few minutes ago, she had put a sign up outside my mom's door that said "Absolute quiet, Patient needs rest". I know she wrote that for me, not for my mom. I've been Nurse Hollingers patient the last few nights. She said she'd call Carol for me. I really have to buy her some flowers, maybe some chocolates, a fruit basket perhaps. Nurse Hollinger.

(Spotlight fades out and spotlight comes up on upper stage left. We see an older woman, Nanny Reid, sitting in a wheelchair with a young boy on her lap)

VERY YOUNG MIKE:
When's mom coming home?

NANNIE REID:
(Snuggles the boy in close)

She'll be home soon Mikey. You just keep watching out the window there and you'll see her coming down the street.

VERY YOUNG MIKE:
(Excited)

Oh good! I can't wait for mommy to get home!

(Straining to see out the imaginary window)

Mom! Mom! Where are you?

NANNIE REID:
Oh sweetie, you just have to learn a little patience is all.

VERY YOUNG MIKE:
(Sees his mother through the imaginary window, starts waving wildly)

Mom! It's mom! There she is! I see her! Mom! Mom! Mom!

(Fade to black as spotlight comes up on Mike, lower stage right, he is looking over at where the other spotlight faded out then looks back at the audience)

MIKE LANE:
(Smiles)

Do any of you women in the audience know how much a boy can love his mother? Do you really? I mean, the love between a mother and daughter truly is special. The love a boy has for his mother is something unique, it's completely different. It's something that can't be described. Do you know, do any of you know what one secret a boy has? That every little boy has? Do any of you know who a boy's first crush, I mean his VERY first crush, is on?

(Spotlight stays up on Mike Lane as spotlight upper centre stage comes up on Mom In Her 30's, flipping through a phone book, Very Young Mike is on his knees on the floor, holding her pant leg and looking up at her)

VERY YOUNG MIKE:
Mom?

MOM IN HER 20'S:
Yes hun?

VERY YOUNG MIKE:
Will you marry me?

MOM IN HER 20'S:
(Looks down at him confused)

What did you say?

VERY YOUNG MIKE:
Will you stop growing older? Will you wait for me to catch up to you so I can marry you and then we can grow old together?

MOM IN HER 20'S:
(Squats down on her toes, lifts Very Young Mike's face up by putting her hand under his chin, pauses, then lovingly says)

I just might do that.

(Kisses Very Young Mike slowly on the forehead. As the spotlight fades to black, we hear Very Young Mike say)

VERY YOUNG MIKE:
I love you mom.

MIKE LANE:
(Is now holding the slippers from his pocket and is smiling)

Ask you husbands. Ask your boyfriends. Ask them who their first crush was on. They'll tell you some girls name from second or third grade.

(Laughs to himself)

Gail Brown. *(Pause)* They think it's wrong for their first crush to be their mother. It sounds, wrong. It sounds silly. Then ask them who the first woman was that they loved. The very first time they felt love. It wasn't their father, it wasn't an aunt or uncle. It wasn't even their grand parents. The very first woman that a boy loves, is his mother. The very first crush a boy has, is the crush he has on his mother. The very first woman a boy wishes he could marry is the woman that he desperately wants to tell to stop growing older *(pause)* so that he can catch up *(pause)* and grow old with her.

(Fights back some tears, face slowly turns to a bit of a grimace)

A man once said that love is blind but it is also cruel,
it's harsh, it's demanding, it changes.

(A new spotlight comes up beside the one Mike Lane Is in. He walks over to it as the one he was in fades to black)

Did you ever wish your mother was dead? I mean really, did you every wish your mother was dead? I did. Oh stop it. Just stop yourselves.

(Mike is getting angry now)

Yeah, she was my mother. I loved her because she was my mother. It came to give me a very perverted sense of what love was too. Yeah, you're probably sitting there now wondering how on earth anyone could wish their mother was dead. You have no idea what I went through with that woman. So stop judging me okay? Look at me.

(holds his arms up and turns around)

Just look at me will you? Do you see any deformities on my body? Do you see any missing limbs? Do you see any scars on my body? Do you?

(Now yelling)

Do you see any scars on my body?

(Pauses, gets hold of himself just a bit, returns to a normal level of voice but still very angry, starts pounding the centre of his chest with a pointed fingers)

That's because the damn scars that woman left are in here!

(Now saying it slower emphasizing each word)

The scars – she left – are in – here!

(Spotlight on Mike Lane extinguishes, spotlight lower stage left comes up on Mom In Her 30's looking down as though she is talking to a child but none is there, facing towards where Mike Lane was on the stage)

MOM IN HER 30'S:
(Yelling)

Why can't you do what you're damn well told? Why?
How many times do I have to tell you to do it?

(Pauses, voice goes to normal level, she turns around and folds her arms)

If you're not doing what I asked you to do, I guess
that means you don't really love mommy.

(Pause as though child is responding)

Nope. You don't love mommy.

(Pause as though child is responding)

If you really did love mommy then you'd do what she

asked you to, if you really loved mommy.

(Pause as though child is responding)

Since you don't love mommy any more, I guess mommy is just going to have to go find a new little boy that WILL love his mommy.

(Pause as though child is responding)

Nope, you can just go find a home somewhere else, I'm going to go find a new little boy who will love his mommy and do what she asks him to.

(She then walks quickly out of the spotlight. As the spotlight goes completely dark, we hear a child from backstage scream "Mommy!!")

(Spotlight quickly comes up on Mike Lane where he was, he is on his knees, hands over his head, rocking back and forth)

MIKE LANE:
(Screams)

Mommy!!!!!

(Pause, then more quieter as he keeps rocking, lifts his head to look where Mommy In Her 30's had been standing, he is practically begging through his tears)

Mommy, I do love you. I do love you mom. Please don't stop loving me. I'll be good. I promise I will. Please don't stop loving me mommy. Please.

(Spotlight comes up on lower stage left, we see Mom In Her 30's and Seven Year Old Mike. She is on the floor cross legged and he is sitting in her lap, they are reading a Dr. Seuss book together, preferably "Rosie The Police Horse" if you can find it. We can hear them reading it together quietly)

MIKE LANE:

(Continues rocking for a moment, then looks up a bit dazed and confused, realizes where he is, wipes his eyes, stays sitting on the floor and turns to face the audience, sitting with his legs crossed. He pulls out her slippers from his pocket and starts playing with them in his hands)

It wasn't like that all the time. Not all the time. I have a lot of good memories from when I was a kid. Some. They're hard to remember. I've been making the effort lately though. As I sat there by her bed, Mom became a bit like a kid again. She was telling me things that happened thirty, forty years ago like they had happened just that afternoon. There was a lot she didn't tell me. There was a lot about my mothers life I had to pick up from snatches of over heard conversation. You know, reading between the lines. I had to piece things together I had heard over a number of years. Snippets of things she said, that Nannie Reid said. Things that my aunts and uncles and cousins said. Yeah, typical mid 20th century family. Don't air the dirty laundry. Don't talk about the things that would bring discredit to the family name, oh God no, not that! Don't even mention them in the house. Like if we don't talk about it, God won't know about it. If we don't talk about it, it never happened!

(Pauses, looks down then up, taps himself
on the chest and say sarcastically)

Look at me, the bastard, the living reminder that you screwed up.

(Looks down and fiddles with the slippers a moment,
then looks back up at the audience with a vague smile)

My mom didn't tell me everything. She didn't tell me
how hard it was at first.

(Mom In Her 30's and Seven Year Old Mike get up and
walk out of their spotlight, it fades to black)

Mom got dealt a shitty hand from the get go. She kept getting bowls full of lemons from life. *(pause)* We drank a lot of lemonade when I was growing up.

(Spotlight on Mike Lane fades to black. Spotlight on upper centre stage comes up, Nannie Reid is sitting there in her wheelchair, worrying a tissue with her fingers)

UNCLE #1:
(Walks into the spotlight, is angry)

Keep it? What do you mean she wants to keep it?

(Walks out of the spotlight)

UNCLE #2:
(Walks into the spotlight from opposite side, is angry)

There is no way in hell she is going to disgrace
our family name, thundering hell!

(Walks out of the spotlight)

UNCLE #1:
(Walks into the spotlight from opposite side, is angry)

She got herself pregnant and now she wants to bring it home?

(Walks out of the spotlight)

UNCLE #2:
(Walks into the spotlight from opposite side, is angry)

I don't know where you went wrong with her. You didn't do a very good job with her Ma. What the hell did you teach her anyways?

(Walks out of the spotlight)

UNCLE #1:
(Walks into the spotlight from opposite side, is angry)

Why the hell does she want to bring
that bastard child into this house?

(Walks out of the spotlight)

UNCLE #2:
(Walks into the spotlight from opposite side, is angry)

She doesn't give a friggin' damned about us. About any of us! She couldn't keep her legs closed and now she wants to saddle us with that little bastard she's having? No friggin' way.

(Walks out of the spotlight)

UNCLE #1:
(Walks into the spotlight from opposite side, is angry)

You do whatever the hell you want. I want nothing to do
with that whore or that whore's child.

(Walks out of the spotlight)

(Nannie Reid cries into the palm of one hand, resting on the arm of the wheel-chair, her other hand raises and drops a couple times in frustration)

MOM IN HER 20'S:
(Walks in holding a baby wrapped up, to her shoulder. Looks fearfully at Nanny Reid, places one hand on her shoulder)

Mom? Do you want me to go away?

NANNY REID:
*(Reaches up and pats Mom In Her 20's hand on
her shoulder, shakes her head)*

No child.

(Looks up at her, looks her in the face)

You're my daughter. You'll always...

*(Trails off, looks at the baby, sits up and straightens herself,
lifts her chin and proudly says)*

You and my grand son will always have a home with me no matter
what anyone says. They can all go to hell.

*(Spotlight fades to black.
Spotlight comes up on Mike Lane forward stage right)*

MIKE LANE:
(Smiling)

Ahh Nannie. In all my years on this earth I have never met a woman like
you. No one who could even hold a candle to the incredible power that
you were.
(Looking upwards)

I remember you every day Nannie, you have never left me, even after
being dead so many years, you never left me. God I loved that woman.
True to her word, I was welcomed into her home with my Mom.

*(Spotlight comes up on upper stage left on the two uncles. They are silently
having a very animated discussion with one another. Mike Lane looks over his
shoulder at them, turns back to the audience, jerks his thumb over his shoulder at them and continues speaking.)*

Those two assholes, my uncles, her brothers, didn't speak to my mother or have anything to do with me for over a year. It wasn't till after my
mother met and married the man who became my father, that they
finally came around. My mom forgave them. That was what you did
back then. People apologized. You forgave them. No matter what they

had done to you. That was what you did back then.

(Spotlight on the uncles fades to black. Spotlight comes up beside the one Mike is in, as he crosses into it, the previous one he was in fades to black)

Did any of you ever have love turn sour but remain? Have any of you loved a person so hard on one hand but hated them so hard on the other? Have any of you ever wanted to kill a person and love them like mad at the same time? Have you? Do any of you know what that's like?

(Breaks down into tears, spotlight goes dim but not totally out, spotlight comes up on lower stage right, Mom In Her 20's is sitting on the floor, rocking a baby in her arms, softly singing Frere Jacques. She continues to do this until the queue for her to exit the stage)

MOM IN HER 30'S:
(Walks into the spotlight and stops to stand behind Mom In Her 20's. She leans over with hands on her knees and says)

I love you Mikey

MIKE LANE:
(Standing in his half light spotlight)

Do any of you know the power of your words,
the power they have over a child?

MOM IN HER 30'S:
(Stands up and crosses her arms, speaks in a harsh voice)

Of course it's my fault. It's always my fault. The first time
I do anything right will be when I take my last breath.

MIKE LANE:
Do any of you know how long a child can
remember the words he hears?

MOM IN HER 30'S:

(Leans over the two on the floor again, hands on her knees)

You're mommy's handsome little boy. Mommy loves you so much.

MIKE LANE:

Do you people not realize that a child can take the important words he hears in his childhood and carry those words with him till the day he dies?

MOM IN HER 30'S:

(Stands up and crosses her arms, speaking harshly)

You and you're damned father can go to hell.
I might as well just be dead.

MIKE LANE:

Can you even conceive the effect those words have?

MOM IN HER 30'S:

(Leans over the two on the floor again, hands on knees)

You know Mikey, some people think we're more like brother and sister than mother and son. You really are my best friend in the world, you know that Mike? You really are.

*(Reaches down over the shoulder of Mom In Her 20's
and caresses the baby's cheek)*

MIKE LANE:

Do you people not realize how your words can change a persons future, can change how their life will play out? Do you people not realize that the things you say to your child are going to affect every relationship they ever have?

MOM IN HER 30'S:

(Stands up and crosses her arms)

You don't really love mommy do you. If you did love mommy, you'd do what she says. I guess you're just going to have to go away so that mommy can find a new little boy that really will love his mommy.

MIKE LANE:

And when we are sitting there, looking back at the horrible things our parents did, at how mean our parents were, while were thinking about all the nasty things they said to us, the hurtful things, has any one of you ever stopped to really think about was going on inside of them?

MOM IN HER 30'S:

(Collapses behind Mom In Her 20's, to her knees, puts her arms around Mom In Her 20's, who does not react to it, starts crying uncontrollably and after a moment lifts her head to look right in the spotlight and screams)

What am I doing??

(Cries uncontrollably, hugging Mom In Her 20's as the spotlight fades to black, both exit).

(Spotlight comes up full on Mike Lane, he is composed and trying to smile)

MIKE LANE:

My mother had a wicked sense of humour. Well, she thought she did. It sometimes seemed though, that she was the only one that understood it. One of her favourites was when she was reading the obituaries. *(Laughs)* Didn't all the older folks read the obituaries back then? Anyways, she'd be reading them and look at me and say "Oh Mikey, look at this!". I'd look over her shoulder and ask her what she wanted me to see. She'd say, "Look, everyone died in alphabetical order again."

(Laughs quietly to himself)

I remember, when we were getting ready to go to city hall the day I married my first wife, we were all at our apartment. My pregnant intended, my mother in law to be, my shotgun totting father in law to be, my sister in law and brother in law to be, my step father, my two step sisters, they were all standing around in the living room with me. We were talking about the plans for how the rest of the day was going to proceed. My mom was in the bedroom getting changed. Then she comes out into the living room, she was just wearing her panties and a bra. She said she needed her purse. Then she looked at my father in law to be, grabbed her right tit, shook it at him and said, "How do you like that Elmer, does that do it for ya?". Then she started laughing and walked back into the bedroom. Everyone just looked at me. They looked at me. *(pause)* Have you ever wanted the ground to open up and swallow you whole?

(Pause, Mike looks down at the ground, puts his hands in his pocket, digs one of his toes at the ground for a few moments, then looks back up at the audience)
Oh, did I tell you that I've been married four times?

(Spotlight on Mike Lane extinguishes. Spot light comes up on upper stage left. Nanny Reid is sitting in her wheel chair, Mom In Her 30's is standing at a hot plate heating up some Jiffy Pop popcorn, the kind in the foil plate that balloons up.)

NANNY REID:
(Laughing and talking to Mom In Her 30's. For this sequence, talks at random to Mom In Her 30's about innocuous stuff a little boy would do, coming in to get ready for lunch, being covered in dirt, not listening properly, making her laugh with stupid kid jokes. The exact dialogue is not important so long as it's low key and harmless)

(Jiffy Pop starts popping, as the tempo increases
Mom In Her 30's starts yelling)

MOM IN HER 30'S:
Ow! Ow! Help! Help Me! I've been shot! I've been shot! Help Me! Someone's shot me!

(Mom in her 30's turns off the hot plate, puts the Jiffy Pop on the cold element, then quickly lays down on the floor and closes her eyes).

SEVEN YEAR OLD MIKE:
(Comes running full tilt into the spotlight, sees his mother on the floor, runs over to her, gets down on his knees and grabs her hand)

Mom! Mom! Wake up mommy! Wake up mom!

(Starts crying)

Mommy!! Please don't die! I don't want you to die!
Wake up mommy! Wake up mom!

(Now screaming)

Wake up! Wake up! I'll be good! I promise I'll be good.

(Now quieter and crying as he talks)

I'm sorry I didn't listen to you mom! I don't want you to die. Please don't die mommy, please, please, please wake up! Wake up! Wake up! I love you mom! I love you mom!

*(Starts sobbing and crying hard for a few moments,
bent over his mother and holding on to her)*

MOM IN HER 30'S:
*(Opens her eyes and exchanges a glance with Nanny Reid.
Reaches up and hugs Mikey and sits up)*

Now, now Mike. There's no need to cry. Mom was just funnin' ya.
I was just joking with ya.

SEVEN YEAR OLD MIKE:
*(Jumps up and backs away from her. Wipes his eyes
with his sleeve, pauses, then screams at her)*

That's not funny! I thought you were dead!
That's not funny mom!

(Turns and runs from the spotlight. Spotlight fades to black)

MIKE LANE:
(Spotlight comes back up on Mike Lane)

Yeah, my mom started her vaudeville career early. She was a real peach. I spent the next five years of my life terrified my mother was going to die and leave me all alone. How's that for telling your kid you love him. Have you ever sat and watched your seven year old son cry himself to sleep, night after night, terrified he'd wake up in the morning and his mother wouldn't be there?

(Original spotlight comes up beside the one Mike is in, he crosses into it as the one he leaves fades to black. Blue spotlight comes up on lower stage left. We see Mom In Her 20's sitting on the floor again, holding the baby wrapped up, faintly singing a lullaby again)

You must think by now that I grew up with an evil and vile woman. I didn't, really. *(Pause)* The word "quit" was not in my mothers vocabulary.

MOM IN HER 20'S:
*(Tears in her eyes, anger on her face and in her voice,
holds the baby closer and looks up at the audience)*

Give you up for adoption? They'll never
take you away from me.

NEVER!

*(Mom In Her 20's looks back down at the baby, starts rocking back
and forth and faintly singing a lullaby again)*

MIKE LANE:

My dad worked as a barber for years. When that wasn't bringing in enough money, he quit it. Closed his shop. Started driving a truck. My mom always worked. She worked some pretty shitty jobs too.

(Looks over at Mom In Her 20's and smiles. Spotlight on Mom In Her 20's fades to black as he is looking at her)

She new how to take care of business, that woman. I grew up on a small Island on the east coast, in New Brunswick. President Roosevelt had his summer cottage there, even though the Island was Canadian. Campobello Island. It was a big tourist draw. Very quaint and picturesque for the tourists.

(Spotlight comes up half way on upper middle stage. Mom In Her 20's and Mikes Father are standing there, slow dancing together, on the same spot, kiss once in a while)

The tourists used to like to drive down to the government wharf and take pictures of the boats, of the men unloading them. My mom worked in a fish plant for a number of summers. Not in the winter, it always closed in the winter and the folks all went on pogey for half the year. It was a Sardine plant. They were contracted by Brunswick sardines. She sat there on the assembly line, snipping off heads and tails, stuffing the fish into the tin. One to the left, one to the right. One to the left, one to the right. One to the left, one to the right. Ten hours a day. Six days a week. Weeks on end. I remember her coming home from work. She always smelled like Sardines. It seemed like we couldn't get the smell of sardines out of the house those summers.

(Looks at his fingers, clenches them a couple times)

I remember her hands. They were always red and raw. She always had tape around her fingers. Bandages weren't good enough. You still might seep blood out of the edges. Instead, the women used white medical tape to wrap up their fingers when they cut them.

*(Holds up one hand and uses the other to make
a winding motion around one of the fingers)*

The tape was easy to go on, sure, but I still remember my mom stand-ing at the sink, crying as she tried to pull the tape off the cuts. They would cut their fingers once in a while with the scissors they snipped the heads and tails off with. One to the left, one to the right. One to the left, one to the right. They cut them on the edges of the sharp cans they put the sardines into. One to the left, one to the right.

(Stops making the winding motion and drops his hands)

Can you imagine? Spending the summer on an assembly line in a sar-dine factory, sweltering heat, fetid fish stink all around you, no air con-ditioning, big vats going to cook the fish, big walk-in ovens going to cook them again inside the cans? Any of you folks ever eat sardines? Did any of you ever eat Brunswick sardines? Which kind did you like? The kind in oil? The kind in tomato sauce? The kind in mustard?

(Raises his hand)

I liked the mustard ones myself. Always had them on crackers. Well, my point is, if any of you good folks had Brunswick sardines back in the early seventies, there's a good chance that my mom may have packed that tin for you. *(Pause)* Think about that next time you pass a tin of sar-dines in the grocery store. Think about the woman who packed that tin and what her life is like. Think about the little boy that might be waiting at home for the mostest beautiful women in the world to walk in the door. The woman who packed that tin of sardines.

(Mikes Father and Mom In Her 20's leave their spotlight, they walk back into it as the spotlight widens a bit. They are carrying a small table. There are two plates with a sandwich and potato chips on each plate. Mikes Father then gets a chair and sets it one side. Mikes Father and Mom In Her 20's take each others hand and walk out of the spotlight. Brief pause. Nannie Reid wheels into the table on the side with the plate with no chair and Seven Year Old Mike walks up and sits in the chair that is on the opposite side of the table. Takes a

bite of his sandwich, does an eye arching look at his grandmothers sandwich. She is slowly eating a potato chip. Seven Year Old Mike jumps out of the chair and runs out of the spotlight, can hear him talking in the dark)

SEVEN YEAR OLD MIKE:
Hello? Yes. We're just eating lunch.
You want to talk to Nannie? Okay.

(Seven Year Old Mike runs back into the spotlight and hops back up in his chair.)

Nannie, mom's on the phone.

NANNY REID:
(Looks over her shoulder confused)
What? I didn't hear the phone ring.

SEVEN YEAR OLD MIKE:
Yes it did, I just talked to her. It's sitting on the hall table.
She wants to talk to you.

NANNIE REID:
Are you having fun with me?

SEVEN YEAR OLD MIKE:
No! She's on the phone. Don't talk to her, I don't care.

(Nannie Reid has a confused look on her face and turns around in her wheelchair, wheels out of the spotlight. As soon as she leaves the spotlight, Seven Year Old Mike jumps up on his knees on his chair, reaches over and pulls a big slice of dill pickle out of his grandmothers sandwich, holds it high over his tilted back head and lowers it into his mouth. He then sits down, chews the pickle then takes a bite of his sandwich.)

NANNY REID:
(Speaking from the darkness)
Hello? Hello? Are you there dear? Hello?

(Wheels back into the spotlight and to the table)

There was no one on the phone Mikey.

SEVEN YEAR OLD MIKE:
(Shrugs his shoulders and keeps eating)

Dunno. She must have hung up.
You probably took too long to get to the phone.

NANNY REID:
(Picks up her sandwich and takes a bite of it)

(Spotlight fades to black. Spotlight comes up on lower stage right, on Mike Lane. He is smiling and laughing to himself)

MIKE LANE:
God I loved that old woman. Did you see that?

(Pointing behind him to where they were)

Did you see that? *(laughs)* I used to do that to her all the time. All the time! I don't think my grand mother ever managed to eat a slice of dill pickle in her sandwich the whole time she lived with us! I remember, I remember once, for lunch, we were having hamburgers. This time the phone really did ring, she went to answer it and she was only talking a few minutes. While her back was turned, I grabbed the whole hamburger patty out of her bun, stuffed it into my mouth and ate it like a ravenous dog. She wheeled back to the table, I jumped up and said, "I'm all done Nannie, I'm going out side to play" then BANG! Off like a shot, out the door!

(Spotlight comes up behind Mike Lane. Mom In Her 30's is standing there, looking furious, has her arms folded and a wooden spoon sticking up out of her hand and she's slowly wiggling it back and forth. Spotlight fades to black as quick as it came up).

(Mike Lane stops laughing)

I paid for that one.

*(As Mike Lane stands there in the spotlight, puts his hands
in his pocket and looks down at the ground)*

NANNY REID:
(From the darkness)

No! Leave him alone, I'm not hungry, I had enough lunch.

(pause)

Leave him alone!!

(Sound of a young child sobbing softly for a moment)

MIKE LANE:
(Looks up at the audience)

My mom was a trooper. She would have gone to the ends of the earth
for me. You really have no idea what her life was like. What it was like
for us.

*(Spotlight comes up beside the one Mike is in. As he crosses into it,
the spotlight he leaves fades to black)*

My mom. She really was an amazing woman.
She always managed to come through in the end.

*(Spotlight comes up on upper centre stage. Seven Year Old Mike is sitting at
the table, looking bored and colouring in a colouring book with crayons. Mom
In Her 30's is standing behind the table, back to the audience, arms are folded
and head is down. Mike Lane turns in his spotlight to watch this scene as his
spotlight fades to black.)*

SEVEN YEAR OLD MIKE:
Mom, I'm hungry.

MOM IN HER 30'S:
(Pause)

Dinner will be in a few hours Mike.

SEVEN YEAR OLD MIKE:
I know. *(Pause)* I'm hungry.

MOM IN HER 30'S:
Dinner will be soon hun. It won't be long.
Do you want a cold glass of water?

SEVEN YEAR OLD MIKE:
No. *(pause)* Do we have any potato chips?

MOM IN HER 30'S:
(Shakes her head)

No.

SEVEN YEAR OLD MIKE:
(pause, looks up at his mothers back)

Do we have any apples mom?

MOM IN HER 30'S:
(Shakes her head no)

SEVEN YEAR OLD MIKE:
(pause)

Mom?

MOM IN HER 30'S:
(Even though her back is to the audience we can see she is very upset and trying to control herself)

Yes hun?

SEVEN YEAR OLD MIKE:
Can I have a glass of water please?

MOM IN HER 30'S:
(Loses it. Starts crying and sobbing, after a moment of this turns and walks out of the spotlight as she says)

Yes hun.

SEVEN YEAR OLD MIKE:
(Looks at his mother walking away, sad look on his face. Looks down at his colouring book and then starts colouring again.)

(Spotlight fades to black. Spotlight comes up on Mike Lane, lower stage right)

MIKE LANE:
(Is looking at the audience. Half turns and looks back to the darkness where that scene had just been played. Turns back to the audience)

Do we have any Mom's in the audience tonight?

(Peers around into the audience. Looks at his feet, looks up straight out at the audience again.)

I hope none of you ever know the pain that a young mother feels when her child is hungry and she has no food for him. *(Pause)* I hope to Christ none of you mothers ever know that pain she feels, when she realizes that her child understands this and even worse, when her child accepts it as a way of life. *(Pause)* Just like everyone else back then, we had lean times, we had fat times. Unfortunately, there were a lot more lean times than fat times. For all of us.

*(Looks back over his shoulder at that spot on the stage
and then looks back at the audience)*

I lived that one folks. I lived that one too many times to count. You'd be surprised how far a cold glass of water will go to curbing your hunger pains. *(Pause)* For a while.

(Spotlight fades to black on Mike Lane. Spotlight comes up on lower centre stage. Mom In Her 30's is standing there. She has one arm across her stomach, her other hand is held up to her forehead, head tilted forward a bit, she is crying. We hear Mikes Father and the two Uncle's singing from the darkness, the opening to Simon & Garfunkel's "Bridge Over Troubled Waters")

MIKES FATHER, UNCLE #1, UNCLE #2
"When you're weary,
Feeling small,
When tears are in your eyes,
I will dry them all,
I'm on your side, whoah, when times get rough,
And friends just can't be found,
Like a bridge over troubled water,
I will lay me down,
Like a bridge over troubled water,
I will lay me down."

(Mike Lane walks into her spotlight. He stands there a moment, then leans in and kisses her softly on the temple. She does not react to his presence. He puts his hand on her shoulder. In a voice that is soft and full of love he says)

MIKE LANE
Don't cry mom.

(We hear Mikes Father and the two Uncle's continue to sing from the darkness as Mike Lane stands there with his hand on her shoulder, looking at her, stroking her hair once in a while.)

MIKES FATHER, UNCLE #1, UNCLE #2
"When you're down and out,
When you're on the street,
When evening falls so hard,
I will comfort you,
I'll take your part, whoa, when darkness comes,
And pain is all around,
Like a bridge over troubled water,
I will lay me down,
Like a bridge over troubled water,
I will lay me down."

(Looks down at her feet and sees a glass of water. He reaches down and picks it up. Looks at it for a moment and slowly drinks the whole glass. As he finished the glass of water, he smacks his lips and makes a satisfied "ahhhh" sound afterwards. Looks at his mother again, then looks at the glass. Sets it back down at her feet. He stands up, looks lovingly at her for a moment as his one hand strokes her back and says)

MIKE LANE
I'm not hungry any more.

(Pause, kisses her on the temple again, then says)

I had a cold glass of water.

(Mike turns around and walks out of her spotlight, she stands there continuing her silent crying as we hear Mikes Father and the two Uncle's continue to sing)

MIKES FATHER, UNCLE #1, UNCLE #2
"Sail on silver girl,
Sail on by,
Your time has come to shine,
All your dreams are on their way,
See how they shine, whoa, if you need a friend,
I'm sailing right behind,

Like a bridge over troubled water,
I will ease your mind,
Like a bridge over troubled water,
I will ease your mind."

(Spotlight fades to black, spotlight comes up on Mike Lane lower stage right.. Mike stands there a moment, lost in a memory. Then turns to the front and addresses the audience again)

MIKE LANE

It didn't matter that there was nothing in the cupboards. It didn't matter. Every day. Every time that little scene repeated itself, mom always managed to have dinner on the table. I know that she rationed. She kept stuff up out of sight in the cupboards so that she could have dinner on the table. I guess it hurt her less if she couldn't see the food in plain view when she knew she had to hold back from giving me any, for a few hours. Wouldn't have done anyone any good to eat it for a snack and then have nothing left for dinner. Nope. That woman had the courage of a lion and an iron will that would put most of you people to shame. Do any of you out there really understand how good you have it? Mom always had dinner on the table. Sometimes dinner wasn't anything to write home about. But at least after dinner, I didn't have to drink a cold glass of water. *(Pause)* There were many nights that dinner consisted of boiled cabbage, a can of peas and some potatoes. Yep, ate lots of potatoes when I was a kid. You could get a fifty pound bag for less than two dollars back then. Woman like my mom could really stretch out that bag of potatoes too. Well, near the bottom of the bag...

(Pause, shakes his head with an apprehensive look on his face)

...sometimes the bottom of the bag got interesting. I remember more than once, sitting there at the table, eating my dinner. My dad would have a piece of potato on his fork, he'd pause a second, then put it on the edge of his plate. I'd be eating away and I'd see mom's fork stab a piece of potato on my plate, then put it on the side of her plate. I'd say something like, "No mom". She'd just say, "Eat your dinner Mikey" then carry on eating hers like nothing happened. *(Pause)* Yeah, I saw the bad bits on the potatoes. I saw the dark spots. I'd have eaten them though. I was hungry. Besides, even back then, young as I was, I had a clue what my mother went through to put dinner on the table. I wasn't going to insult her efforts by turning up my nose. Yeah, Mom, I'd have eaten that potato. I'd have eaten it just so I didn't have to see that look on your face when you had to take a piece of spoiled food off your sons plate *(pause)* while he was eating.

(Pause, brightens up)

Saturdays were always the same. Four o'clock was Bugs Bunny. Four-thirty was "Lost In Space"

(Starts flapping his arms around like Robbie the Robot)

"Danger Will Robinson! Danger! Danger!

(Stops, smiles)

Ahhhh, five o'clock. Five o'clock on Saturday afternoon was the moment I waited all week for. On Saturday afternoons at five o'clock, on channel two, WGLZ from Bangor Maine, I got to go exploring. I travelled to far and distant places and saw things that no other person on earth had ever seen. Me and my friends had adventures like no one else ever had. You know my friends. Jim Kirk, Dr. McCoy, Scottie, Mr. Spock. We travelled the universe at light speed. *(Pause)* At least in Gene Roddenberry's universe, nobody ever had to drink a glass of cold water because they were hungry. Every Saturday night was baked beans night. Baked beans with molasses if things weren't too lean. My dad and I always put mustard on our baked beans. I still make baked beans myself once in a while. I'm about the only one that eats them. My wives never understood why I'd have to dab away a tear or two when I was eating them. I was remembering her. Mom. One of the things that Star Trek teaches it's fans is I.D.I.C. That stands for "Infinite Diversity in Infinite Combinations". Sort of like my mom's cooking. There were three things she made that I went crazy for. I thought they were the absolute best things on the face of the earth. One was "Burger and Sauce". My mom would fry up some hamburger then mix up the sauce with it and serve it over boiled potatoes, sometimes over bread if there were no potatoes left. That sauce, I've tried making it but just can't get it right. Water, a little flour, a little cornstarch. Heat it, keep stirring. That's it. We didn't have spices back then. They were too expensive. Pepper was about the only spice we had. Salt. Another favourite of mine was Hobo's Dinner. A can of peas, a can of mushroom soup. Mix them together with a bit of water, heat them up and then serve them over toast. I like two slices of toast, *(laughs quietly)* a double-decker surprise! The other thing she made was Mulligan stew. Of course, we only had Mulligan stew during the fat times. It was easy to make. She'd boil up a big pot of macaroni. She'd sauté some green pepper, mushrooms, onions and ground beef. Then she'd mix it all together. She'd throw in a can of Campbell's tomato soup and then a block of cheese that she had cut into small cubes. Old cheese of course. Old Nippy if she could get it. She's stir it up and then let it sit about ten minutes. She cooked it in this big old two handled pot she had. She called it her dutch oven. You know how she served it from the pot? Coffee mug. She'd take a coffee mug and use that to ladle it onto the plates. My wife wonders why I can't seem to be able to throw out any of the two dozen coffee mugs I have in the cupboard at home. I can't.

(Spotlight on Mike Lane fades to black.
Blue spotlight comes up lower stage left)

MOM IN HER 20'S:
(Clutches the baby to her shoulder, faces directly
at the audience with dark anger in her face)

I'll never give you up. They'll never take you away from me.

(Spotlight goes down fast as another spotlight
comes up on upper stage left)

MOM IN HER 30'S:
(Angry and bordering on tears)

Of course it's my fault, it's always my fault The first time I do anything right will be when I take my last breath.

(Spotlight goes down fast as blue spotlight comes back up lower stage left fast)

MOM IN HER 20'S:

(Still holding the baby, looks into it's face, kisses it, holds it back to her shoulder. Looks forward and up a little bit as though she is thinking about something, sways back and forth a bit, patting the baby's back, after a few moments she slowly says)

Infinite Diversity in Infinite Combinations.

(Spotlight fades to black fast. Spotlight comes up on centre stage. We see a table, Mikes Father, Mom In Her 30's and Seven Year Old Mike are sitting at it, slowly eating dinner. Tensions are running high, Mikes Father knows a storm is brewing and is pussy footing around it, Mom In Her 30's is pissed beyond words but not doing a very good job of hiding it from the child, Seven Year Old Mike is reacting to each exchange, starts getting more and more despondent with the exchange between his parents, he is sitting back to the audience).

MIKES FATHER:
Did you talk to Jeannie today?

MOM IN HER 30'S:
Yes.

MIKES FATHER:
Are you going over there tomorrow.

MOM IN HER 30'S:
Does it matter?

MIKES FATHER:
I was thinking of going to Lubec with Jed.

[Writers note: The above mentioned Lubec is in the state of Maine, not in Texas. It is pronounced "Loo-BECK" and not "LA-Bock" as it is in Texas]

MOM IN HER 30'S:
(Glares at Mikes Father for a moment, returns to eating)

MIKES FATHER:
Do you want me to pick up anything for you?

MOM IN HER 30'S:
Like you care.

MIKES FATHER:
Dammit woman, I just asked if you wanted anything.

MOM IN HER 30'S:
Don't pretend with me. I know what you and Jed do.

MIKES FATHER:
(getting mad)

You don't know anything.

MOM IN HER 30'S:
(voices are rising)

I know a hell of a lot more than you think I do.

MIKES FATHER:
What then? What the hell do you know so well?

MOM IN HER 30'S:
I know that I hate you for what you're doing to me.

SEVEN YEAR OLD MIKE:
(Jumps up from his chair, throws his fork hard onto the table. Starts crying as he yells at his parents)

Stop it! Stop fighting! I can't take it any more, you two
are fighting all the time and I can't take it any more!

(Mikes Father just looks on here, surprised, startled, not sure what to do)

MOM IN HER 30'S:
*(Grabs Seven Year Old Mike by the arm with an angry look,
is loud and harsh, shakes him a bit)*

Sit down and shut up and eat your dinner!

SEVEN YEAR OLD MIKE
(Crying hard and openly now)

I don't want any of your damned dinner! I just want you two to stop
fighting! You're always fighting! Just stop it! Stop it!

MOM IN HER 30'S:
*(Stands up leaning over the table, shakes Seven Year Old Mike by
the arm even harder, trying to force him back into the chair)*

Stop your yelling and stop your crying! Stop your crying!
Sit down and eat your friggin' dinner!

SEVEN YEAR OLD MIKE:
(Breaks free from her grip, steps back just out of her reach)

No! I can't eat when I'm crying!

(Runs out of the spotlight crying and holding his fists to his eyes)

*(Can still hear Seven Year Old Mike crying in the dark as Mom In Her 30's
glares at Mikes Father, pushes her chair back and walks into the darkness.
Mikes Father looks dumbfounded, put his elbows in the table and lowers his
face into his hands. Childs crying stops. Fade to black).*

(Blue spotlight comes up on lower stage right. Mom In Her 20's is

standing there holding her baby to her shoulder.)

MOM IN HER 20'S:
(Speaking softly)

They'll never take you away from me.
They'll never take you away from me.

(Spotlight fades to black fast. Red spotlight comes up fast on upper stage right. Mom In Her 30's is standing there crying.)

MOM IN HER 30'S:
(Screams in rage with fists clenched then says)

The first time I do anything right will be when I take my last breath.

(Spotlight fades to black fast. Yellow spotlight comes up fast on upper stage left. Seven Year Old Mike is curled up on the floor in the fetal position crying. Light stays on him for three seconds in this pose then spotlight fades to black fast. Blue spotlight comes up on upper stage right fast [yes, where Mom In Her 30's was previously].)

MOM IN HER 20'S:
(Clutching the baby to her shoulder, head lowered onto the baby's head, rocking in a swaying motion with him)

Never *(pause)* Never *(pause)* Never *(pause)* Never

(Longer pause as she sways a few times, then she stops movement, looks up and directly out at the audience and screams loudly)

NEVER!!!!

(Spotlight extinguishes. Spotlight on upper stage left comes up. Seven Year Old Mike is sitting cross legged, flipping the pages of a comic book but not really seeing the pages. While we are watching this, blue spotlight comes back up on upper stage right. Mom In Her 20's is still there, swaying with the baby.)

MOM IN HER 20'S:

(Looks around at the floor, she is now barefoot. Looks up at the audience with a confused look on her face)

Where are my slippers?

(Spotlight extinguishes)

MOM IN HER 30'S:

(Walks into the spotlight upper stage left with Seven Year Old Mike, has a plate of food in her hand. She looks at him for a moment flipping the pages of the comic book)

Mike?

SEVEN YEAR OLD MIKE:

(stops flipping pages, sniffles, does not look at her)

Yeah Mom?

MOM IN HER 30'S:

(Sits on the floor next to him and hands him the plate of food)

Here Mike, I brought your dinner for you, eat some for me, okay?

SEVEN YEAR OLD MIKE:

(Puts a bit of food in his mouth and chews it slowly for a moment. Looks up at his mother and then back at his plate)

I'm sorry I yelled at you Mom.

MOM IN HER 30'S:

(Fights back tears, puts her arm gently around his shoulders)

I know hun. It's okay. Everyone was a little upset.

SEVEN YEAR OLD MIKE:

(Chews a moment on another bit of food)

Mom? Why do you and dad fight so much?
Don't you love each other any more?

MOM IN HER 30'S:
(Takes a deep breath, looks at the ceiling for a moment
then down at Seven Year Old Mike)

I do love your dad Mike. I love you too. It's just that, well, sometimes things aren't always simple with adults. Sometimes we can love each other and still not like each other very much. Right now, right now I don't like your daddy very much but I still love him. I still love you too.

SEVEN YEAR OLD MIKE:
Why are you mad at him?

MOM IN HER 30'S:
Well Mike, that's between your daddy and me. We'll work it out though. We always have before, right?

SEVEN YEAR OLD MIKE:
(pauses, then nods his head)

(Spotlight comes up slowly on lower stage right, Mike Lane is standing there with his hands folded in front of him, watching this scene unfold)

MOM IN HER 30'S:
(Looks up and arches her neck a bit to look out the imaginary window)

Look Mike, the other kids are outside playing.
Why don't you go outside and play with them?

SEVEN YEAR OLD MIKE:
(Shakes his head)

No, I just want to stay here.

MOM IN HER 30'S:

Come on Mike. Let me have your plate. I'll warm it up later for you. Why don't you go outside and play with your friends for a while. You can stay up a little bit later tonight.

SEVEN YEAR OLD MIKE:

(Thinks about it a minute, then shakes his head)

No, I'd rather stay here with you.

MOM IN HER 30'S:

(Fights back tears, slowly rubs Seven Year Old Mikes back with the hand that was on his shoulders)

I know Mike. Mom loves you. I have to go do dishes and tidy some things up, go outside and have some fun. Please?

SEVEN YEAR OLD MIKE:

(Looks at his mom, looks back at his plate, pauses a moment. Hands her the plate, stands up and starts to walk out of the spotlight. Stops at the edge of the spotlight and turns around, looking at his mother.)

I love you mom.

(He turns around and exits the spotlight. Mom In Her 30's breaks down in silent sobs. Fade to black)

(Blue spotlight comes up on upper stage right.)

MOM IN HER 20'S:

(Clutching the baby to her shoulder, swaying side to side, slowly sings)

Hush little baby, please don't cry.
Momma's gonna sing you a lull-a-by.

(Spotlight fades to black Spotlight comes up on lower stage right.)

MIKE LANE:
(Turns to the audience slowly looks around)

Never before and never since, have I ever felt so loved by mother as I did, sitting there on the floor of my bedroom, with her rubbing my back. She ponied up that day. It would have been easy for her to wallow in that pit of misery she was swimming through. It would have been easy for her to stay down in the kitchen and leave me on my own. She didn't though. She knew she had some music to face. She put on her Stetson, she climbed up in the saddle and she ponied up. She faced something she didn't want to have to face, she did something very hard. It took a lot of guts for her to walk into my bedroom and face me after what had happened at the table.

MOM IN HER 20'S:
(Singing slowly and quietly from the darkness)

Hush little baby, please don't cry.
Momma's gonna sing you a lull-a-by.

MIKE LANE:
*(Looks down at his hands, then at his watch.
Looks up in surprise at the audience.)*

Oh gee, look at that. I didn't realize so much time had gone by.

(Pats down his pockets and looks around then looks back at the audience)

I could really go for a smoke right now. Mmm, a coffee too. Any of you want one? Anyone need a pee break?

*(Looks at his watch, claps his hands together, then
rubs them together, a smile on his face)*

Let's take a break shall we? Say what, fifteen minutes? That good for you folks? Tim? Tim? Can we get the house lights please?

SEVEN YEAR OLD MIKE:
(Singing from the darkness)

Hush my momma, please don't cry.
Baby's gonna sing you a lull-a-by.

MIKE LANE:
(Face freezes. Fade to black.)

END OF ACT 1

ACT II

(Spotlight comes up on centre stage. Mike Lane is standing there with a Styrofoam coffee cup in his hand. He is looking around at the stage behind him. Spotlight catches him off guard and he turns around quickly, almost spills some coffee.)

MIKE LANE:
(Surprised look on his face)

Oh, we're back? Already? Geez.

(Looks around for what to do with the coffee cup. Walks out of the spotlight to the side of the stage sets down his coffee cup and returns to the spotlight. Looks inquisitively out at the audience)

Everyone good? Have a coffee? We all settled?

(Pause, waits a moment for a reply from the audience)

Good. Let's continue shall we?

(Spotlight on Mike Lane fades to black. Spotlight comes up on upper stage right. We see Mom In Her 30's and Seven Year Old Mike sitting at the table. Seven Year Old Mike is reading slowly and haltingly from Dr. Seuss. Mom is sitting at the adjacent side of the table, sipping her coffee and listening to Mike while looking lovingly at him. She helps him with a word once in a while. He reads two pages of the book. At this point, they continue reading silently as spotlight lower stage right comes up on Mike Lane)

One of the things my mom believed in was education. There was nothing in my world that was more important to her than for me to do well in school. I did well too. Right up until high school. *(Laughs)* Girls!

(Goes sombre)

And my dad died. When I was fifteen.

(Pause, then looks over his shoulder at the two of them at the table)

Every day when I came home from school, right up to grade seven, it was the same thing. That entire first hour that I was home was study time. I wasn't allowed to go play, watch TV or do anything until I had done an hour's worth of homework. If the teachers didn't send enough homework with me, Mom made me create my own. She'd make up math problems for me. She would ask me to help figure out some simple kitchen math with her. A lot of the times she'd make me read. I didn't mind. It made her happy. I'd have done anything to make the mostest beautiful woman in the whole world have a smile on her face. Besides, life was a lot easier when she was happy. A lot easier. I'd read from my school text books. If I didn't have a text book or got bored with it, she'd make me pick out one of the volumes of the Funk and Wagnalls Encyclopaedia and read from it.

(Pause as he smiles at the memory)

That was one of the things my mom gave me. That thirst to learn. That thirst to read. I was a voracious reader. By the time I was in grade two, I was reading stuff like the Little House series by Laura Ingles Wilder. I had read all of her books by the end of grade three.

(Looks over his shoulder at the two at the table and back at the audience)

When I think back to my child hood, that's one of the images that always comes to mind.

(Jerks thumb over his shoulder at them)

Sitting at the kitchen table with my mom, reading to her. She'd either sit there with me or busy herself with cleaning or cooking. She always paid attention though. Near the end of "study time", she'd take what I had been working on or reading, then sit there at the table with me and test me on it. She'd give me an oral quiz. She'd ask me all sorts of stuff about what I had been reading or the homework I had been doing. She never missed a trick. Not just two or three questions either. I'm talking ten or twenty questions.

(Spotlight on Mom In Her 30's and Seven Year Old Mike fades to black. Mike Lane pauses, holds up one of his hands in front of him, concentrates on it furiously, then slowly extends his first finger. He looks at it from all sides slowly. He then haltingly lifts his other hand in the air, pauses a moment, then makes a wrapping motion around the extended finger as his tongue comes out the side of his mouth, licking his lips in concentration like a young child, makes six or seven winds around his finger and then says while still focussing his eyes on his fingers. He is wrapping imaginary medical tape around his finger tip.)

My mom wanted me to have a real chance. My mom didn't want me to be trapped in the life she had been caught up in.

*(Mike Lane continues the wrapping motion twice more.
He stops, hands held in place, he looks directly out at the audience)*

My mom wanted to make sure that I knew where my slippers were.

(Spotlight extinguishes on Mike Lane. Red spotlight comes up on upper stage left. Mom In Her 30's is standing there, her arms are folded and she looks pissed off)

MOM IN HER 30'S:
(Says venomously)

The first time I do anything right will be when I take my last breath.

*(Spotlight fades quickly to black. Spotlight comes up
on Mike Lane lower stage right)*

MIKE LANE:
(Smiling)

You remember that? You know when the last time
that I heard that was? I had just turned 15.

(Spotlight fades to black on Mike Lane)

(Red spotlight comes up on upper stage left on Mom In Her 40's standing there, her arms are folded and she looks pissed off. She is facing where Mike Lane was)

MOM IN HER 40'S:
(Says venomously)

Yes of course it's all my fault. The last time I do anything right will be when I take my last breath.

(Red spotlight comes up on lower stage right on Teenage Mike, he is looking across stage at Mom In Her 40's)

TEENAGE MIKE:
(Pissed off)

Then do it.

MOM IN HER 40'S:
(Looks surprised)

What?

TEENAGE MIKE:
Go ahead and do it.

MOM IN HER 40'S:
Do what?

TEENAGE MIKE:
Just do it. Take your last breath. Go ahead.

MOM IN HER 40'S:
(Shocked)

How can you say that?

TEENAGE MIKE:
(Pissed off and almost shouting)

Because I'm sick and tired of hearing you say that. I've listened to it all my life. So why don't you either go ahead and do it or just shut up stop saying it.

(Teenage Mike turns around and storms out of the spotlight, that spotlight then fades to black. Mom In her 40's is standing there with her mouth agape in shock and then her spotlight fades to black)

(Blue spotlight comes up on lower stage left. Mom In Her 20's is standing there swaying back and forth with the baby held to her shoulder, she is singing softly)

MOM IN HER 20'S:
Hush little baby, please don't cry.
Momma's gonna sing you a lullaby.

(Stops swaying and looks out at the audience)

They'll never take you away from me.

*(Spotlight fades to black. Spotlight comes up on
lower stage right on Mike Lane)*

MIKE LANE:
(Smiling still)

Yep, it worked. She never said that or anything like that again. My dad was there. He was sitting at the table.

(Laughs to himself)

I thought his eyes were going to pop out of his head. No one ever talked to her like that! No one! Not even him! He told me later that once the blood started moving in his body again, he had to get up and go down to the basement because he knew that if he laughed out loud in her face, hell would have had to be paid. *(Laughs)* My mom lightened up a lot on my dad after that too. Guess it did us both good.

(Spotlight fades to black on Mike Lane. Red spotlight comes up on upper stage left. We see Mikes Father, Mom In Her 30's and the two uncles. Mikes Father is wearing underwear and a T-Shirt. He is coming out of a severe diabetic reaction, he keeps rolling his eyes up into his head and making unintelligible grunting and moaning noises. The two uncles are on each side of him and trying to restrain him. Mom In Her 30's is in front of him and also trying to restrain him. He seems to have the strength of ten men. The mom and two uncles are scared and straining quite hard, you can hear it in their voices.)

MOM IN HER 30'S:
Hold him! Don't let go of him! Get him back onto the chesterfield.

UNCLE #1:
Damn it! He's nuts!

MOM IN HER 30'S:
No! He's coming out of an insulin reaction! When he gets to the point he's comatose, coming out of the coma always does this!

UNCLE #1:
How often does this happen?!

MOM IN HER 30'S:
Never if he pays attention and takes care of himself! *(pause)*
This usually happens a couple times a year.

UNCLE #1:
What happened?! What caused it?!

MOM IN HER 30'S:
Who knows! He didn't eat lunch yesterday and
he only picked at his breakfast!

UNCLE #2:
I saw him eating a chocolate bar this morning, would that do it?

(Mikes Father gets uncle #1 in a headlock and squeezes.
Uncle #1 starts yelling in fear and in pain.)

UNCLE #1:
Get him off! Get him off! It hurts! It hurts! Get him off!

MOM IN HER 30'S:
(Grabs Mikes Fathers arm and starts yanking
at it to get it off uncle #1's neck)

Let go of him! Let go of him!

(Starts pounding on Mike's Fathers chest and shoulders)

Let go of him! You're hurting him! Let go of him!

MIKES FATHER:
(Lets go of Uncle #1 and slips out of the grip of Uncle #2. Throws his arms around Mom In Her 30's still making horrid noises, he grips her very, very tight with one arm. The other arm grabs her wrist and bends her arm around behind her back).

MOM IN HER 30'S:
Ahhhhhh! You're hurting me! You're hurting me! Get him off me! Get him off me! He's breaking my arm! Ahhhhhh!

UNCLE #1 AND UNCLE #2:
(Both grab him and after a bit of a struggle, wrestle him off Mom In Her 30's. She takes a breath and goes back into struggling with him. Spotlight fades to black. Spotlight comes up on lower stage right on Mike Lane.)

MIKE LANE:
You know, it was a real eye opener for me. Looking back over the years and finally using the understanding of an adults eyes to try and come

to terms with the experiences of a child. It opened up new avenue's of understanding to the woman who I *(Pause)*, who I misunderstood for so long.

(Spotlight fades to black. Spotlight comes up on upper centre stage on Mom In Her 30's. She is sitting on a kitchen chair and talking on a phone that she is holding on her knee).

MOM IN HER 30'S:

Hi mom, Happy Easter! Yes, Mikes fine. Yes, his fathers fine. Yes, I'm fine. What? No, I didn't get it. I'll get him to go to the post office on his way home tomorrow. What? No, no I'm okay.

(Starts crying. Cries haltingly through the rest of the conversation)

Oh mom. I haven't seen anyone since December. Because of the snow! It started snowing on the 27th and it's March now and it's only finally starting to melt enough to get around easily. No. No I haven't. I haven't been able to get the car out or go anywhere. Yeah, he walks through it to get to work. No, Mikey can get through it and get to the bus stop. Because there's no one around here my age! All my friends are too far away to walk to in this weather. No mom. No! I've tried! I can't get out to end of the lane even. Mom, the only people I've seen since the end of December are Eddie and Mikey, the only ones! I'm going stir crazy here mom. It's the same every winter. Every winter!! No, I have no job in the winter mom, you know that. The plant doesn't work in the winter and the burger stand doesn't open until the spring. No, he gets groceries at the store on his way home from work. Sometimes he takes the toboggan to bring them home on. Mom, you don't understand. It's been three months! Three months since I've seen another human being besides the two of them! I'm going nuts. I'm losing it with them, I'm yelling at them, I'm just.... I just don't care about anything anymore.

(Spotlight fades to black. Spotlight comes up on lower stage left on Seven Year Old Mike, Teenage Mike and Mike Lane pacing back and forth in opposite directions, Teenage Mike is behind Seven Year Old Mike, Mike Lane is behind Teenage Mike, one repeats the other. They are rubbing their hands together

as they are extremely worried and are devising a plan to deal with a situation)

MIKE LANE then **TEENAGE MIKE** then **SEVEN YEAR OLD MIKE**:
What do I do? What do I do? I've got to be fast.
I've got to think ahead.

MIKE LANE then **TEENAGE MIKE** then **SEVEN YEAR OLD MIKE**:
If I know what she wants first, she won't yell at me.

MIKE LANE then **TEENAGE MIKE** then **SEVEN YEAR OLD MIKE**:
If I do it ahead of time, she'll love me more.

MIKE LANE then **TEENAGE MIKE** then **SEVEN YEAR OLD MIKE**:
If I can guess what she wants, if I can always guess what
she wants, she'll love me more.

MIKE LANE then **TEENAGE MIKE** then **SEVEN YEAR OLD MIKE**:
I've got to be fast.

MIKE LANE then **TEENAGE MIKE** then **SEVEN YEAR OLD MIKE**:
I've got to think ahead.

MIKE LANE then **TEENAGE MIKE** then **SEVEN YEAR OLD MIKE**:
I've got to be perfect.

MIKE LANE then **TEENAGE MIKE** then **SEVEN YEAR OLD MIKE**:
I need to make her love me. I can't have her stop loving me.

MIKE LANE then **TEENAGE MIKE** then **SEVEN YEAR OLD MIKE**:
I need to be perfect. I need to be her perfect little boy.

MIKE LANE then **TEENAGE MIKE** then **SEVEN YEAR OLD MIKE**:
I don't want her to find another little boy. I want to be her little boy.

MIKE LANE then **TEENAGE MIKE** then **SEVEN YEAR OLD MIKE**:
I want her to love me. I want her to love ME.

MIKE LANE then **TEENAGE MIKE** then **SEVEN YEAR OLD MIKE**:
I've got to be fast. I've got to think ahead.

MIKE LANE then **TEENAGE MIKE** then **SEVEN YEAR OLD MIKE**:
(Stop and look at each other, then in unison)

I've got to be perfect.

(Spotlight fades to black. Blue spotlight comes up on lower stage left. Mom In Her 20's is standing there swaying back and forth for a few seconds, humming to herself, with the baby held to her shoulder. She then sings softly)

MOM IN HER 20'S:
Hush little baby, please don't cry.
Momma's gonna sing you a lullaby.

(Spotlight fades to black. Blue spotlight comes up on upper centre stage. Mom In Her 40's and Mikes Father are dancing to the song "In The Living Years" by Mike and the Mechanics. Mikes father is wearing blue work pants and work shirt again. They dance for two minutes and then the song fades down as the spotlight fades to black. NOTE: Sound person should pause the song at the point it fades out as it will be restarted at that point later)

(Yellow spotlight comes up on upper stage left. We see Mom In Her 40's and Teenage Mike standing there hugging each other and crying. Wipe their own tears and each others tears once in a while and go back to hugging)

MIKE LANE:
On April 30th, 1991 I got up a bit late for school. I'd been up late the night before. I was in a kind of teenager surly mood. You know those. Right? The kind of mood your kid has where you think to yourself, oh good, if I take him out I can make another one that looks just like him. *(Chuckles)* My dad was working night shift at Baxter Dairies. He was the security guard. He'd worked there for years. Actually, he worked for Parrtown Security but it was the Baxter Dairy site he always worked at. So I got up late and had to have a quick bowl of cereal. He had just finished giving himself his morning insulin, he was tired, I could see he

was tired. Ginger, my mom's dog, was sitting on his lap. He was stroking her soft ginger coloured hair as he tried to talk to me. I say "tried to" because I wasn't being particularly conversational. In fact, if the truth be known, I was being an asshole. He couldn't say anything right. I was crabbing at him and bitching at everything he said. I could see in his face that it was hurting him but I really was kind of powerless to stop myself. I had given into that mind space where you are so over tired you think you have the right to treat people anyway that you want to. This didn't take long, only a few minutes. I threw on my jacket and my bag, slammed the door and stormed up the driveway. That was when it hit me. The man I loved, the man who had changed over the years and become so much better a person than he had been when we were all younger, this man who I looked up to was sitting at the table and hurting because I had been such a prick. I turned around and walked back to the house.

(Mom In Her 40's walks out of the spotlight, leaving
Teenage Mike standing and crying by himself)

I knew that I had to apologize to him and tell him that I loved him. So I unlocked the door and walked into the house. As I stepped into the hallway, he wasn't in the kitchen. I turned around and saw his bedroom door closing. I paused for a moment. He was so tired, he had worked all night, I figured he needed a good sleep more than anything. *(Pause)* I was also kind of afraid to face him after the way I had just treated him. Knowing their parents, as kids do, I knew that some time would dull the pain I had caused. I headed back out the door and said, "I'll tell him later". *(Pause)* "I'll tell him later". Four words. Just four words. The worst four words I've ever spoken. Of all the words I've spoken in my life, I'd trade my entire life just to take those four words back. I'd give up anything I have to go back to that hallway, knock on his door and when he opened it, put my arms around him and tell him how much I loved him and how much he means to me. Just four words. "I'll tell him later".

(Spotlight fades to black on Mike Lane and on Teenage Mike. Spotlight comes up on upper stage right, we see Mom In Her 40's sitting at the table with a cup of coffee held between both of her hands. She sits there staring into it,

once in a while she takes a sip, then sets it down and holds it with both hands again. Every once in a while, breaks into a few tears then wipes them away and recomposes herself)

(Spotlight comes up on lower stage left)

TEENAGE MIKE:
(Walks into the spotlight with his hands in his pockets on lower stage left. Is looking downwards most of the time as though in shame, only looks at the audience once in a while)

The city bus passed right by our house going to the bus stop. I saw the police car there and the ambulance there. I knew that something had happened to my dad. I looked at one of the guys from school on the bus and said, "My dad's dead". He just stared at me. He didn't know what to say. I wanted to run to the house but I couldn't. I knew that if I ran to the house, I'd find out too soon. I didn't want to find out at all. I didn't want to hear it. For a few seconds I thought about staying on the bus and not going home at all. Then I thought my Mom had to be home and I knew she'd need me. I walked slowly to the house but when I got to the bottom of the stairs, I ran up them and ran in the door. When I opened the door, right in front of me, two cops were standing there. An old guy and a rookie. The rookie looked at me, looked right at me. Looked me right in the eyes. I'd always heard about people turning white but I'd never seen it, till then.

(Jerks thumb over to where Mike Lane was standing)

Ask the old guy, both of us still remember what
that kids face looked like. That cop.

(Mom In Her 30's and Mom In Her 20's walk into the upper stage right spotlight with Mom In Her 40's. They stand behind her and each one puts a hand on her shoulder as they look over and watch Teenage mike talking. Their hands can rub her shoulders or back slightly as he talks, comforting her but she never reacts to them.)

Every ounce of colour drained out of his face and he kind of slumped back against the wall. I guess he was standing there thinking about his dad and what it would be like if he'd been the one to have that happen. Then I walked in. I guess I mirrored his fears to him. I dunno. That sounds good. I'll stick with it. When I saw that look in the rookies face, my hands opened. Everything I was carrying just fell to the floor.

(Spotlight extinguishes on the three women)

I heard my mom say, "Oh no, my son's home". She came running into the living room and put her arms around me. She was crying. She said, "You have to be strong for me. He's gone".

(Mom In Her 40's, Mom In Her 30's, Mom In Her 20's walk into Teenage Mikes spotlight and put their arms around him and look at him. Teenage Mike then continues)

We stood there that way for a couple of minutes. I couldn't believe it. He was gone. He was really gone. Even though my dad had cleaned up his act a lot, he was still a pain in my mothers ass a lot of the time. I blamed him for a lot of the suffering my mother had done. I knew then that his death meant a lot of that pain would be gone. I also knew that it was going to open up a lot of new pain for her. I guess that all I could see was the surface, the end results of stuff. I guess that I never, ever really saw how much my mom did love my dad. It would take me until I was almost 40 to really understand that. From that moment it would take me twenty-five years and three wives to really understand un-conditional love. *(Pause)* As we stood there, the rookie cop went outside. I saw his partner out of the corner of my eye pretending he'd forgotten his notebook. He told his partner to go see if it was in the police car. I looked at the older cop. Looked in his eyes. That was the first time I understood what it was like to have a complete stranger use a single look to extend compassion and strength. He wanted to come hug me too. He wanted to come hug me and tell me it would be okay. I could see it. I could see the redness in his eyes and that he was fighting back some tears as well. Then the ambulance guys wheeled the stretcher down the hallway, past the door to the living room. I knew it was going to happen. I said, "Wait, I want to see him". The big cop said, "No son, you don't" and he put his arm out to stop me from moving any further. I hated him for that. Years later, I would come to understand why he did that.

(The three women join hands and walk out of the spotlight)

The worst part of my dad dying was that it meant I was all alone with her. There wasn't a buffer there anymore. It was just me and her.

(Spotlight fades to black. Spotlight on lower stage right comes up on Mike Lane who is looking at where Teenage Mike had been)

MIKE LANE:
He's right.

(Looks down, turns and looks out at the audience)

I do still remember what that rookie looked like. For whatever reason, that guys face is etched permanently in my memory.

(Spotlight fades to black. Blue spotlight comes up on upper centre stage as the sound on the song fades up, starting from where it left off. Mom In Her 40's and Teenage Mike are dancing to the song. They continue to dance together slowly until the song ends and then the spotlight fades to black)

(Spotlight fades up on lower stage right on Mike Lane)

MIKE LANE:
You know, for a long time I couldn't listen to that song. I heard it once not long after my dad died. I really listened to the words. Every time I heard it, tears would come to my eyes and I'd start sobbing. It wasn't until I was in my 30's that I resolved the feelings surrounding my fathers death and those four words I spoke. I finally got to a point where I knew I didn't need his forgiveness, I needed to forgive myself. *(Pause)* Listen to the song sometime. It's a beautiful song.

(Spotlight fades to black. Spotlight comes up on upper stage right. Teenage Mike and Mom In Her 40's are sitting at the table playing cards, they are talking and laughing once in a while)

MIKE LANE:
(Walks into the spotlight with them and stands beside them, he is looking at the audience, they do not react to his presence)

The years after my fathers death weren't any easier. They were different. They weren't easier. I did stop hearing a lot of the stuff mom used to say. I didn't forget it though. The memory of it still hurt. My mom and I did start spending a lot more time together.

(Leans over and looks at Teenage Mikes cards in his hands. Walks behind Mom In Her 40's and peers over her shoulder to look at her cards. He reaches out and taps the top edge of one of her cards. Not reacting directly to Mike Lane, she takes that card and moves it to another position in the cards in her hand. Mike walks back to the side of the table and looks smiling at the audience)

I can't even begin to guess at the number of hours my mom and I sat at the table playing cards. It became an almost nightly thing. We actually did it so much that I got sick of it. I'd pretend I had homework so that I didn't have to sit there. The foot rubs too. My mom worked a lot, almost every day. She'd be on her feet all day and get home and quite often she got me to rub her feet with hand cream. I hated doing that but I did it. By watching my mom after my fathers passing, I got to understand the word determination. I really got to understand what it meant to take care of business. I also understood that I was about the only entertainment my mother had. It wasn't easy on her. She was paying a mortgage, paying bills, buying food and raising a teenage son all on a single income. She didn't have any left to play with for herself, except maybe Bingo once in a while. That fall, the year my dad died. I got a job at the nursing home where my mom worked. I got a job washing dishes every day after school and on the weekends. Some days I'd wash dishes, other days I'd bus the tables. On weekends I'd work three shifts. Breakfast, lunch and supper. That was my teenagers money for going out with my friends and stuff. I was even able to kick in once in a while for groceries and stuff. Once I got my license, I did my best to always keep gas in the car so she wouldn't have to worry about that. She'd give me cash once in a while. She liked to do that. It made her feel good. More often than not, any cash she gave me either went into the gas tank or got snuck back into her purse or in to her coat pocket where she'd find it and think she had forgotten about it. She never knew it was me doing that.

(Mike walks out of the spotlight he is sharing, spotlight comes up on lower stage right as spotlight on upper stage right fades to black as Mike Lane walks into the spotlight on lower stage right)

My mom and I have had a strained relationship over the years. I never called her as much as she would have liked. I never visited her as much as she'd like. I've dealt with depression. I had a bit of a booze problem for a while. Successful relationships have not been my forte but I'm getting better with those. It wasn't until I was in my 30's that I decided it was time to start working on all that shit from my childhood, to figure out why I was the way I was and to, well, fix myself. I wish I had done it a lot earlier in my life. Maybe mom and I would have had a better relationship through those years. I had a lot of anger in me, a lot of resentment. I blamed her for a lot of stuff in my life. I always thought she was the one responsible for me being the way I was. It was kind of shocking when someone pointed out to me what an amazingly good person I was, on the whole. I'm fair, I'm honest to a fault, I'm compassionate and considerate of others. I root for the underdog and have put myself in harm's way more than once to get a friend or stranger out of a dangerous situation. People look up to me and respect me. They value my presence in their lives, they value my opinion. They always consider the uniqueness of my views. I'm the sort of person who can face an adverse situation, hunker down and work his way through it without giving up. I can look at any big pile of poo in a persons life and find the good bits in it. I know that there is nothing that this life can throw at me that I can not handle or not deal with. I also have this ability to never give up, to never give in, to keep plodding forward even when a lot of others would just fall down in a crying heap. I've also got the courage to keep looking at tomorrow with a hopeful smile. Even though there has been a lot of emotional bullshit in my life, I don't transfer that onto other people. I keep smiling. I know that I am responsible for my own happiness and that I can't give up hope. *(Pause)* So yeah, after I learned to really look back in an honest way, I could see that my mother was responsible for me being the way I am. Only now I can credit the good as well as the bad that use to be there. *(Pause)* The only way though, that I could reconcile the present with the past was to make myself revisit the past and really look at my mom back then and really try to understand her. To really find that place of love again for her.

(Spotlight fades to black. Red spotlight comes up on upper stage left.)

MOM IN HER 30'S:
(Bitter, quiet voice and looking down to the side)

The first time I do anything right will be when I take my last breath.

(Spotlight fades to black as blue spotlight fades up on lower stage left.)

MOM IN HER 20'S:
(Stands there swaying side to side, holding the baby in close with her head tucked against it. We see this for about five seconds and then spotlight fades to black.)

(Spotlight comes up on upper stage right, we see the empty table there. We see Mom In Her 30's struggling with Mikes Father. Mom In Her 30's is wearing a cheap but pretty dress a bit too tight for her. Mom In Her 30's can have this clothing change for the snippet above where she appears on her own. She has nothing on her feet in this sequence. Mikes Father is wearing polyester pants and long sleeve polyester dress shirt that is open at the collar, he has on a white t-shirt underneath. She is being pushed backwards into the spotlight, he has an empty beer bottle in his hand. She is trying to push him away. As she speaks he pushes her back against the table, he is making drunken grunting noises, he drops the bottle, he bends her back over the table and is trying to kiss her, his hands are pushing her and pawing at her)

MOM IN HER 30'S:
No! Stop it! Stop it! Please! You're hurting me
you drunk bastard! Stop it!

SEVEN YEAR OLD MIKE:
(Yelling from the darkness and not seen)

What are you doing! What are you doing to my mommy!
Leave her alone! LEAVE HER ALONE!

MOM IN HER 30'S:
*(Whips her head around to face the audience, tears streak her face.
She is screaming almost hysterically)*

Go to your room! Run Mikey! Run! Run to your room!

MIKES FATHER:
*(Looks towards the audience and starts to move off
Mom In Her 30's towards the audience.)*

MOM IN HER 30'S:
(Grabs Mikes Father and pulls him backwards, he turns back to her and continues the attack. She is screaming even more hysterically now. At the same time, spotlight comes up on Mike Lane. He is standing with his eyes screwed shut and his hands over his ears, he is making herky-jerky side to side movements, trying to shut out the sound of the screaming)

GO! GO TO YOUR ROOM! SHUT THE DOOR MIKEY! SHUT THE DOOR
AND PUT YOUR BED AGAINST IT! GO! RUN! RUN MIKEY RUN! DON'T
LET HIM TOUCH YOU! RRUUUUNNNN!!!!

(Screams in pain three times, each one getting lower in volume. Mike Lane with hands still over his ears and eyes shut, screams in unison with her, his voice stays loud. Spotlight fades to black on the parents and on Mike Lane at the same time. Stage is in darkness)

SEVEN YEAR OLD MIKE:
(Screams from the darkness)

Stop hurting my mommy!

(Sobs a couple of times. Then very quietly says)

Stop hurting my mommy.

(Spotlight comes back up on Mike Lane, he is visibly shaken and takes a moment to compose himself. Looks up, puts on an obviously fake smile)

MIKE LANE
Every Saturday night, after I had toured the universe, eaten my baked beans and said hello to the baby sitter, *(then says sarcastically)* they went to the Legion. That was the only place for adults to get entertainment on the Island. The Legion. They played darts. Not those sleek little darts you get nowadays. They used those big old monsters that looked like something you'd drop from the Enola Gay. And they drank. My dad drank. Mom Too. She never touched a drop after my dad died, oddly enough, but back then, she drank as well.

(Spotlight on Mike Lane fades to black. Spotlight on upper stage right comes up again on the table. Blue spotlight on lower stage left comes up on Mom In Her 20's holding the baby close to her, swaying from side to side with the baby, cheek pressed against that baby's head as she looks down and forward as though she wants to cry. Blue spotlight comes up on upper stage left on Mom In Her 40's, she is standing there with her arms folded across her chest and is watching Mom In Her 30's and she also looks as though she wants to cry)

MOM IN HER 30'S:
(Stumbles drunkenly into the spotlight and crashes into the table. Almost falls but then stands up leaning against the table. She looks directly at the audience, uses the table to support herself, she slurs her words a bit as she speaks)

What are you looking at? What? Go to hell. All of you. What do you know.

(Hand over her mouth like she's going to puke, looks down at the floor, gets hold of herself after a moment and looks back up at the audience)

So, you think you can do better? What was I supposed to do? I made a mistake. I got in trouble, okay? Bastard. Didn't want anything to do with me after that. Yeah, I was good for a little fun but then

(Trails off, looks up at the audience and yells)

Stop judging me!

(Staggers around a bit)

What the hell do you know about anything. You all live in your well to do little worlds. You've all got good jobs, happy families, food in your fridge. You don't open you fridge and find a pack of cheap ground beef with maggots crawling out of it. Do you? DO YOU?. You don't live my life. You don't have to do the shit I have to do just to survive from day to day. *(Indignant)* I make it happen. I make sure that there's friggin' food on the table every night and every morning. Lunches are, *(pause)* a suggestion. Stop looking at me.

(tries to make herself a bit more presentable, gives it up as a futile cause)

Love? What's love? Who cares about love. It was the sixties. I was single. I had a child and I was all alone. None of the men I knew wanted anything to do with me after that. None of them. They all just saw me as a good time girl. Someone who put out.

(Starts crying silently, builds to open mouthed crying with her body being wracked with the power of the sobs, does this a few times and then takes a deep breath and screams)

It was only one time! It was only one time!

(Collapses to her knees and sobs a bit more. Now goes into

a pedantic, fearful diatribe, talking very fast)

What am I going to do? Mom looks after him while I work but she won't be around forever. She's already raised three kids, she's in a wheel chair, she's going half blind, her arthritis hurts her, what am I going to do? I can't just do nothing. The boys don't want anything to do with me, they won't help out, I can hardly afford diapers, I can hardly afford to put food on the table, mom's pension doesn't do much to help, I'm sick and tired of washing diapers, I'm sick of the bucket handle breaking and sopping wet shitty diapers going all over the kitchen floor, I'm twenty-four! I'm twenty four, I should be meeting the man of my dreams, I should be meeting my prince charming, I should be getting married in a big old church, riding in a horse drawn carriage like a princess and being whisked away to start a family the RIGHT way. Not this. Not this!!!

(Pauses, then starts crying loud and hard, pounding on her chest, wailing through tears and a running nose)

Why me?? Why me?? It was only one time!
It was only one time! Why me?
What did I do to deserve his hell?

SEVEN YEAR OLD MIKE:
(Speaking from the darkness, not seen)

Mom? Are you okay?

MOM IN HER 30'S:
(Turns to look across the stage as though she is seeing him. Raises her hand, points and starts shaking her finger and yelling at the unseen child, still drunk and slurring a bit, speaking through a hard bout of frustration and rage coming out as crying)

You! Go to your room. Leave me alone!!
Just leave me alone and go to your room!

(Pause as though she is listening to someone. She immediately softens, hands

fall limply to the floor, she looks down at them and with a screwed up face starts crying hard but without sound to the crying as she manages to say)

If you love me, if you love me you'll just
go to your room and leave mommy alone.

(Hangs there, crying quietly)

MOM IN HER 20'S:
(Stops swaying. Turns and looks at Mom In Her 30's. Shakes her head, holds one hand out towards Mom In Her 30's with her fingers stretched as though she is straining to touch her, as she says, tenderly)

They'll never take him away from us. I won't let them.

(Spotlight fades to black on Mom In Her 20's. Mom In Her 30's is still on her knees crying to herself, now she lifts her arms and starts hugging herself as she rocks back and forth. Continues crying and sobbing silently until her queue to exit)

MOM IN HER 40'S:
(Holds one hand out towards Mom In Her 30's with her fingers stretched as though she is straining to touch her as she says with some pride)

They never took him away from us. I didn't let them.

(Spotlight fades to black on Mom In Her 40's)

MIKES FATHER:
*(Singing sweetly from the darkness, verses are from
a song called "Sweet 16")*

Oooo she's all ribbons and curls,
Ooo what a girl!
Eyes that twinkle and shine.
She's sixteen, she's beautiful and she's mine.

You're my baby, you're my pet.
We fell in love on the night we met.
You touched my hand,
My heart went pop,
And oooo when we kissed, we could not stop!

You walked out of my dreams!
Into my arms!
Now you're my angel divine!
You're sixteen, you're beautiful, and you're mine!
Oh You're sixteen .... you're beautiful .... and you're mine!

*(Spotlight on Mom In Her 30's fades to black during
the last line. She exits. Brief pause)*

MIKE LANE:
(Speaking from the darkness)

If my wife saw that, maybe she'd understand why
I hate eating at the kitchen table.

MIKE LANE:
*(Spotlight comes up on Mike Lane, lower stage right. He has a piece of white
rope in his hand and he is using his fingers to make loops, twist a loop, pull
rope through loop, pull rope through that loop, etc. Takes about a minute to
do this as he whistles the "Sweet 16" tune to himself. When he is done, he
holds it up admiringly and then looks out at the audience)*

Getting fidgety? I bet you're wondering what I'm doing with this rope.

*(Reaches in his pocket and takes out a another straight piece of white rope,
holds it up in his other hand, jerks it up and down and says)*

You see, this white rope, this is our life. It has a starting end and it has,
hopefully a great number of years down the length of it, a finishing
end. The starting end and the finishing end, there isn't too much we
can do about those. They are pretty well, well, fixed quantities, if you

will. But you see all that white rope in between the two ends? When we are born, that straight bit of white rope in between the two ends is our life. It's a blank canvass really. We're free to do what we want with it. Well, actually, we find that as we are working on that canvass, other people tend to come up and dab paint on it here and there as well. *(Pause)* I know, I know, I'm mixing metaphors. Just, just bear with me, okay?

*(Drops the looped rope on the floor and starts doing
the same thing with the new piece as he talks)*

You see, it's as we go through life, that we change how that canvass looks. We change the shape of the line of our life, if you will. We have something fun happen, we change the shape of the line. We meet a new person, we change the shape of the line. We do something good for someone, we change the shape of the line. We have someone do something good for us, we change the shape of the line. That's what life is about friends. It's about doing things, day after day, a succession of moments, a collection of experiences that change the shape of our line. Hopefully, we are changing the shape of the line in a good way.

(Goes silent while he finishes the finger work on the line, when he's done, he ties off the bottom, reaches down and picks up the other one on the floor. Lifts them both up, looks at each as he jerks them up and down a bit simultaneously)

Look at that. Two different ropes.

(Holds them in his hands and admires them, looks up at the audience, holds them up sort of like a product shot for all to see)

Two different lives. All sorts of bends and twists and experiences in them.

(Drops one of them to the floor as he holds up the other one)

Now look at this life line. All full of experiences.

You see, this is my life line.

(Looks at it a moment, then starts tying a single knot in it as he says)

She said that the first time she did anything right
would be when she took her last breath.

(Holds up the line for the audience to see the knot with a surprised look on his face. Turns back to the rope and ties another single knot in it as he says)

If you don't love mommy, she'll find another little boy
who does love his mommy...

(Hold the rope up for all to see and as he looks a the audience says)

...and you'll have to go away and never see mommy again.

(looks at the rope sharply and quickly ties another knot in it, then hold is up for approval nodding his head. Looks back at the rope and ties another knot in it as he says)

How about a cold glass of water?

(Holds the rope up for approval, then ties another knot as he says calmly)

Go to your room Mikey, run, hide, put your bed
against the door. Run Mikey Run.

(Hold the rope up for approval, stops and looks at it, ties two more knots in it quickly, then nods his head in approval to himself. Holds the rope in his hand and strokes it, fingering the knots as he says)

You see friends, this rope of our life, isn't just a bunch of pretty loops. It gets knots in it. It gets kinks in it. These knots and kinks are always there. We can choose to spend our time fingering them and playing with them, or, we can look forward. We can look forward on the rope and see all the pretty loops that don't have any knots in them and then do our best not to put any more knots in it. This rope, this is my life. There are a lot more knots in the real one. Lots of them. There is also a whole lot of the rope that has nothing but pretty loops in it. That's my life I have yet to live. You see, for a long time, for a very long time, all I could do was look backwards. I could only look backwards at the knots in the rope. I spent all my time going over them, fingering them, playing with them. All I could see was the knots in my life and how much they hurt me.

(Looks at the rope a moment, then tosses it on his shoulder. Reaches down to the floor and picks up the one he had previously dropped. Looks at it a moment and then ties a single knot as he says)

It was only once, just one time.

(Looks at the knot and holds it up for approval, looks back at the rope and ties another knot as he says)

I want nothing do to with that whore or that whore's child.

(Looks at the rope and ties a second not, then holds it up for approval, looks back at the rope and ties another knot in it as he says)

Stop it, get off of me, you're hurting me.

(Looks at the rope, ties another knot in it as he says)

I don't' have any food in the house, my son is hungry,
I have nothing to give him.

(Looks at the rope a moment, ties another knot in it as he says)

Would you like a glass of cold water?

(Looks at the rope, strokes it once and then fingers each of the knots, his lips are moving but he's talking to himself, hesitates at the end or the rope for a moment, then snaps out of his reverie and looks back at the audience. He

holds the rope up for all to see and says)

This is my mom's rope. You know, for years, whenever I looked at her rope, all I could see was...

(holds up the rope from his shoulder)

...the knots in my own life line. I couldn't see the ones in her life line.

(Pauses and looks at both ropes in his hands, then says)

Would you look at that. I didn't realize she had so many knots.

(Nanny Reid now walking, Mom In Her 40's, Mom In Her 30's, Mom In Her 20's still holding the baby, Teenage Mike and Seven Year Old Mike all enter Mike Lanes spotlight. The women surround him closely and each of them put a hand on him or arm around his waist, Seven Year Old Mike stands in front of him and leans back against him, Teenage Mike stands beside him with his arm around one of the Mom's, Mike Lane does not react to their presence. They are all looking at Mike Lane and looking at the ropes in his hands. Mike Lane holds up the two ropes in front of him, a confused look on his face, it slowly starts to clear, he smiles determinedly to himself and then ties the two ropes together in three knots, one at the top, one at the bottom and one in the middle. Holds the rope up in front of him and speaks to no one in particular)

Look at that. I didn't realize that mom's life line and my life line had so many knots at the same places. I guess I was too busy looking at my own hurts, *(pause)* to see how much she hurt.

(Mike wraps the ropes around the fingers of one hand, then with both hands clutches them into his chest, he stares straight out at the audience and down a bit. One by one, the women move to his front quarter, starting with Nanny Reid , cup his face and kiss him tenderly on the cheek. As each woman does this, she turns, bows her head and walks slowly out of the spotlight. When all the women are gone, Teenage Mike pats him on the shoulder, hugs him briefly and then exits the spotlight, Seven Year Old Mike starts to leave but stops and comes back, he walks up to Mike Lane and tugs on his jacket sleeve. Broken

from his reverie, Mike Lane looks down at him and then bends over, Seven Year Old Mike cups his hands to Mike Lanes ear and whispers something, then the child looks at him and kisses him on the cheek. The child slowly walks out of the spotlight, Mike Lane stands up slowly as he watches the child leave, turns back to the front and looks down at the ropes. He says to the ropes)

I'll miss her too.

(Mike Lane turns and starts to leave but stops, turns back again to the audience. Looks at them a moment, then smiles. He reaches into this jacket pocket and pulls out his mothers slippers. He looks at them a moment and then sets them down in the center of the spotlight. He stands up and looks at them briefly. He then slowly unwraps the knotted cords from his hands. He looks at the cords and slowly fingers the knots one last time. He then gently lays it on top of the slippers. He stands up, then squats down quickly to make sure the slippers are properly aligned. Mike stands up, pauses, looks at the audience and says)

Thank you for listening.

(Mike Lane turns and walks out of the spotlight. The spotlight starts to fade to black as we hear the following sung by the four women, Mike Lane and Seven Year Old Mike)

Frère Jacques,
(Nanny Reid stops singing)
Frère Jacques,
(Mom In Her 40's stops singing)
Dormer-vous?
Dormer-vous?
(Mom In her 30's stops singing)
Sonner le matin,
Sonner le matin,
(Mom In Her 20's stops singing)
Ding-ding-dong,
(this last line said slower and it just Mike Lane that sings it)
Ding-ding-dong
(As the light goes completely black, we hear Mike Lane

say in a strong loud voice)

I love you Mom.

THE END

(We hear recording "Bridge Over Trouble Waters" play low as lights come up on the stage for the curtain call)

NOTE TO THE DIRECTOR

This play calls for no hard sets. That is, no walls or doors. Simply a few props that get moved around by a couple stage hands and by the cast.

As far as the direction goes for the position of spotlights on the stage, feel free to adjust the positions according to the needs of the set-up of your stage. I do ask, however, that you keep the positions relative to one another as they are in this script. While the direction for red and yellow spotlights may be dropped for plain white light, the calls for a blue spotlight really do need a blue spotlight to be most effective.

There are very few clothing changes in this play. This was on purpose. I wanted to maintain a continuity and carry over from one point in their lives to the next. The visual element of the clothes remaining the same achieves this. It also has the added benefit of making the characters and experiences timeless and more focused on the experience itself rather than when the experience occurred.

During the dinner/argument scene, food on the plate should be potatoes and one vegetable, sliced carrots preferred as they aren't likely to roll off the plate. Sandwich in the scene with the dill pickle can be anything, so long as there is a big slice of dill pickle in Nannie Reid's sandwich that Seven Year Old Mike can easily pick out.

Nanny Reid moves her wheelchair by pulling it along with her feet on the floor rather than using her hands to push the wheels.

While I have changed some names and made some events representative, this play is about my life. I'm sure you can understand that it is very important to me that any production of this play be done with the proper respect and gravitas that it deserves. That said, my stage direction in the script is my vision of how this should be performed but is ultimately, up to you, the Director.

PROPERTY LIST

- 60's style kitchen table with two vinyl chairs
- Wheelchair
- Three plates & cutlery
- Four identical pairs of women's slippers
- Telephone Book
- Coffee Mug
- Dr. Seuss Book
- Hotplate
- Jiffy Pop Popcorn
- Tale top telephone (60's style)
- A baby doll wrapped up in a receiving blanket.
- An empty beer bottle
- Hospital Gurney
- Glass Tumbler
- Handkerchief
- Big slice of Dill Pickle for sandwich
- Big wooden spoon
- Colouring book and crayons
- Styrofoam cup with coffee
- Deck of playing cards
- Comic book

SOUND LIST

- "Mother Machree" – John McDermott
- "In The Living Years" – Mike And The Mechanics
- "Bridge over troubled waters" – Simon & Garfunkel

WARDROBE

Mike Lane Three piece suit OR Single breasted suit. Dress shoes.

Mom In Her 20's Polyester Pants that are tight and tapered. Cuffs should be above her ankles. Ideally, a bold colour such as royal blue, red or forest green.

Polyester long sleeve shirt. Turtleneck shirt would be great. Should have horizontal colour stripes with a colour complementary to the pants.

Has a handkerchief on her head like a bonnet. What you would imagine a 1960's woman to wear while doing housework.

Always wears slippers.

Mom In Her 30's Wears straight leg, shapeless polyester pants with an elastic waist. These are utilitarian pants and not fashionable.

A short sleeved blouse, very plain with no decoration.

For Act II, cheap 70's style one piece party dress. Plain, no pattern to it. Is in contrast to what Mike's Father is wearing in that fight scene.

Always wears slippers.

WARDROBE

Mom In Her 40's   Dressed similar to Mom In Her 30's but clothes look more worn. Always wears slippers.

Very Young Mike   Cheap looking clothes. Shorts and pullover striped shirt.

7yr Old Mike   Blue Jeans and a T-Shirt. Sneakers.

Teenage Mike   Cotton pants and button up cotton shirt. Clothes look a bit more expensive than Mom In Her 40's. Not quite stylish but acceptable.

Nanny Reid   Faded cotton sundress and a natty old sweater over top of it.

Mikes Father   Male in his early 30's. Dresses in workman's blue pants, workman's blue shirt, white T-Shirt, construction boots. Wears glasses.

In Act II wears polyester dress pants, polyester dress shirt. Not a fashion statement by any means. Think tacky and you will be dead on

Uncle #1 & #2   Polyester pants and shirt.

White pants, T-Shirt and hospital smock for opening sequence.

PRODUCTION RIGHTS

This play may be produced by any Amateur or Professional group by following the instructions below. A Professional group is determined by one or more actors being compensated beyond personal expenses.

Contact the author to secure production rights. Author will grant each production a 250 Km exclusive rights license for a period of two years from the first performance.

Anyone receiving permission to produce MAMA'S SLIPPERS is required to give credit to the author as sole and exclusive Author of the Play on the title page of all programs distributed in connection with performances of the Play and in all instances in which the title of the Play appears for advertising, publicizing or otherwise exploiting the Play and/or a production thereof. No person, firm or entity may receive credit larger or more prominent than that accorded the Author.

To contact the author, e-mail: jmelanson1965@gmail.com

Amateur Production:

Amateur production companies shall contact the author to determine if licensing is available in their area. Upon agreement with the author to grant licensing, amateur production companies must submit the following:

- Proof of purchase of eleven copies of this script.
- Licensing fee of CDN$50.00
- Venue name, location and seating capacity.
- Date of opening night and length of run.

Amateur productiong companies will be granted permission to print/photocopy the script from an author supplied PDF in sufficient quantity for non-performing production staff.

PRODUCTION RIGHTS

Professional Production:

Professional production companies shall contact the author to determine if licensing is available in their area. Upon agreement with the author to grant licensing, professional production companies must submit the following:

- Proof of purchase of sufficient copies of the script for each actor (except for Very Young Mike) plus all non-performing production staff.
- Licensing fee of CDN$250.00
- Venue name, location and seating capacity.
- Date of opening night and length of run.

NOTE:

Under no circumstance is any production allowed to edit, change, modify, re-write or alter in any way the text of this script for their production.

NOTES

NOTES

NOTES

NOTES

NOTES

NOTES

NOTES

NOTES

NOTES

NOTES

NOTES

www.ingramcontent.com/pod-product-compliance
Lightning Source LLC
Chambersburg PA
CBHW070646030426
42337CB00020B/4183